Others Matter

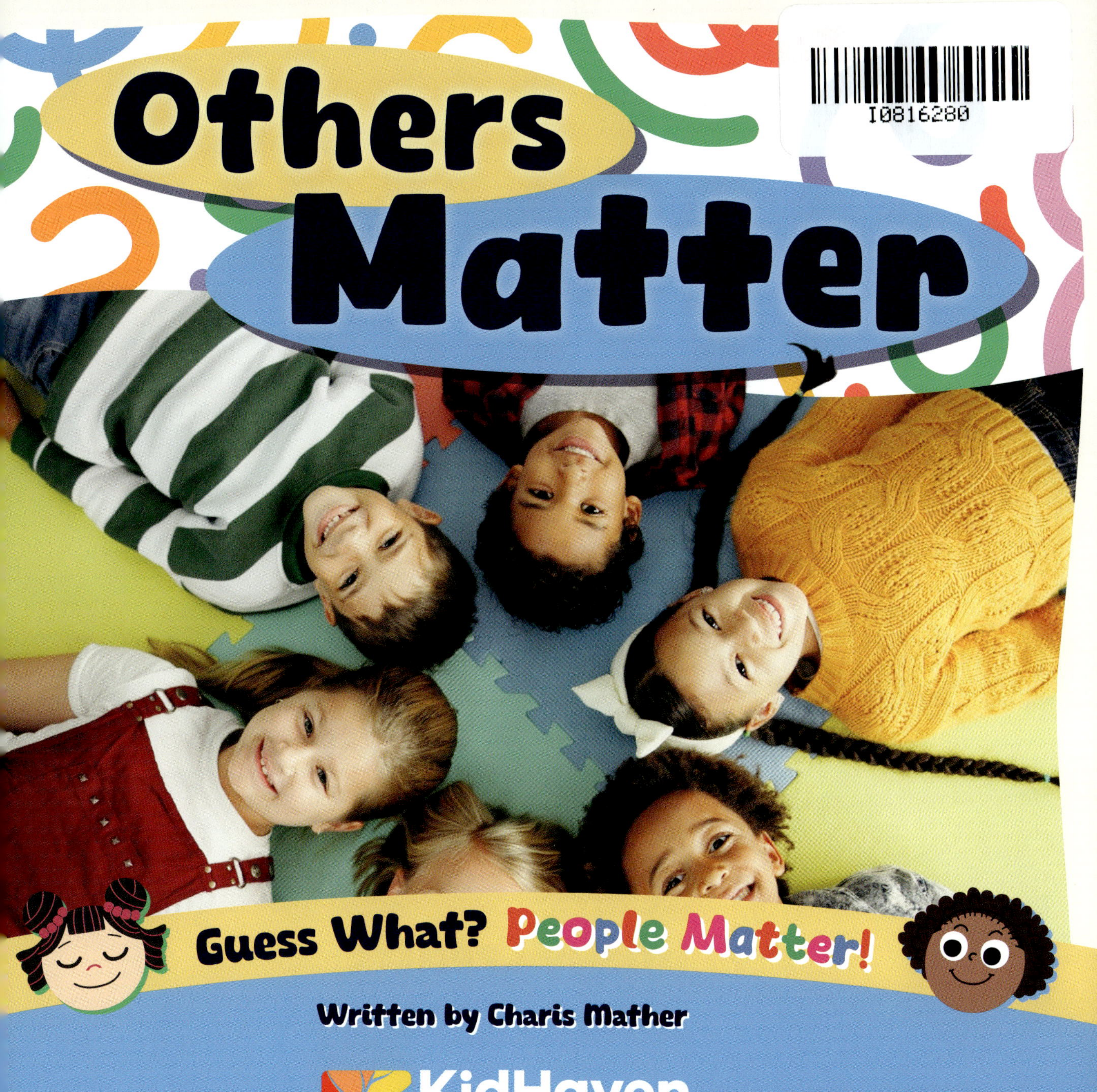

Guess What? People Matter!

Written by Charis Mather

KidHaven Publishing

Published in 2026 by
KidHaven Publishing, an Imprint of
Greenhaven Publishing, LLC
2544 Clinton St., Buffalo, NY 14224

Written by: Charis Mather
Edited by: Noah Leatherland
Designed by: Amelia Harris

All facts, statistics, web addresses, and URLs in this book were verified as valid and accurate at time of writing. No responsibility for any changes to external websites or references can be accepted by either the author or publisher.

Cataloging-in-Publication Data
Names: Mather, Charis.
Title: Others matter / Charis Mather.
Description: Bufalo, New York : Kidhaven Publishing, 2026. | Series: Guess What? People Matter | Includes glossary and index
Identifiers: ISBN 9781534550278 (pbk) | ISBN 9781534550285 (library bound) | ISBN 9781534550292 (ebook)
Subjects: LCSH: Empathy—Juvenile Literature | Kindness –Juvenile Literature | Respect—Juvenile Literature
Classification: LCC HM1035 M38 2026 | DDC 179/.9 --dc25

Manufactured in the United States of America

CPSIA compliance information: Batch #CSKH26
For further information contact Greenhaven Publishing LLC at 1-844-317-7404.

Please visit our website, www.greenhavenpublishing.com.
For a free color catalog of all our high-quality books, call toll free 1-844-317-7404 or fax 1-844-317-7405.

Find us on

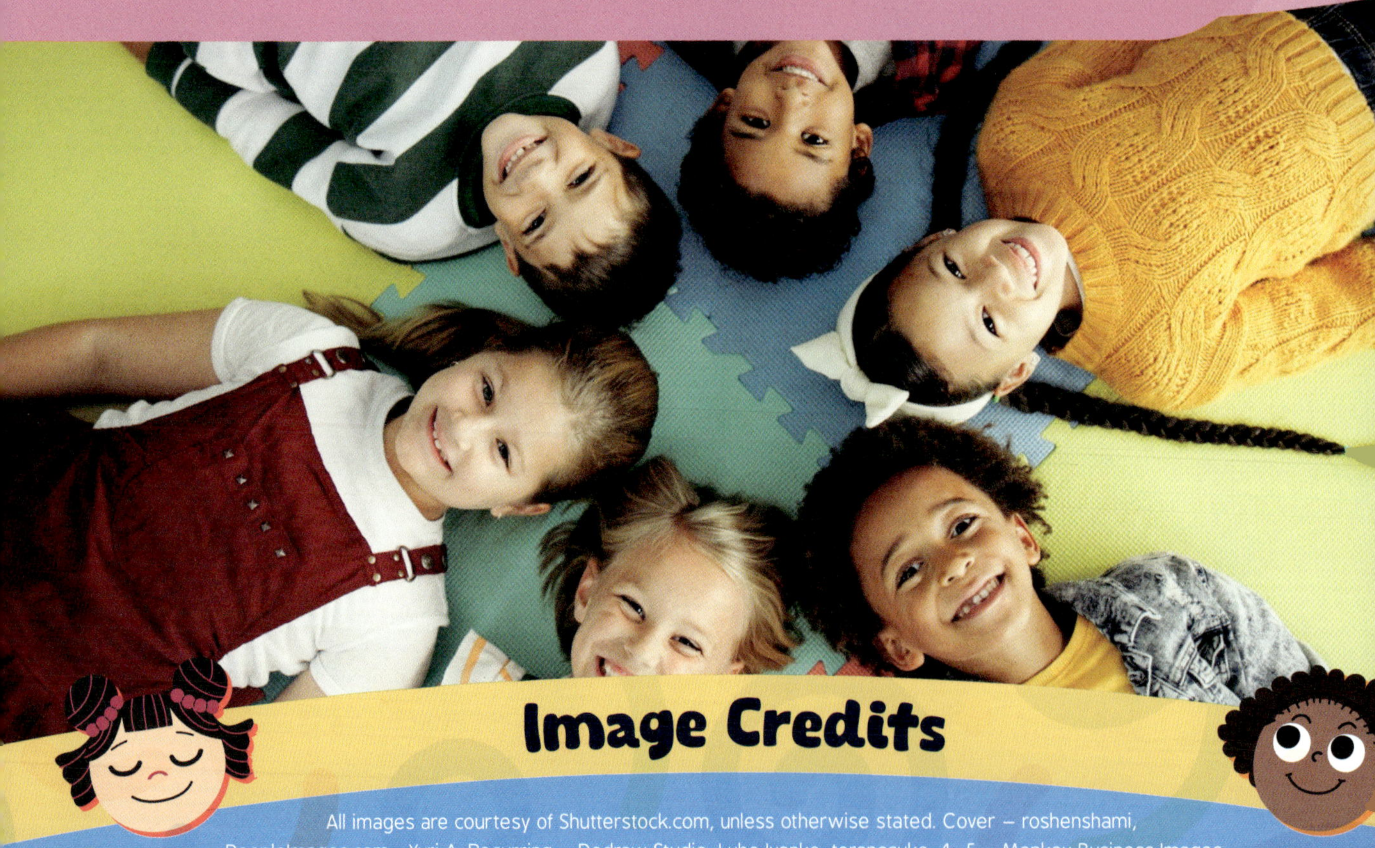

Image Credits

All images are courtesy of Shutterstock.com, unless otherwise stated. Cover – roshenshami, PeopleImages.com - Yuri A. Recurring – Dedraw Studio, Lubo Ivanko, toranosuke. 4–5 – Monkey Business Images, PeopleImages.com - Yuri A. 6–7 – SergiyN, Ground Picture. 8–9 – wavebreakmedia, Iryna Inshyna, KsyushaM. 10–11 – Anna Nahabed, BearFotos. 12–13 – Veja, cheapbooks. 14–15 – AlejandroCarnicero, Jacob Lund, Yuganov Konstantin. 16–17 – MJTH, Robert Kneschke. 18–19 – Pixel-Shot, nakaridore. 20–21 – Hurst Photo, LightField Studios, Roman Samborskyi, Sergey Novikov. 22–23 – Studio Romantic, A3pfamily.

Contents

Words that look like <u>this</u> can be found in the glossary on page 24.

Guess What?

How many people do you know? Probably more than you can count.

And guess what? They all matter!

Everyone you have ever met and will ever meet has their own unique lifestyle and way of thinking.

The world would be much less interesting if it was full of people who were exactly like each other.

No matter how different they are from you, others matter. Everyone is important!

What are some things that make you unique?

Others Matter!

When you hear that others matter, you might think about your friends and family. But "others" means much more than that. It also includes people you might not get along with, or even complete strangers.

In your life, you will meet people who have diverse backgrounds and beliefs. You will meet people who you have lots in common with and people who you have less in common with.

A Wide Worldview

No one has lived the exact same life as you. This means that not everyone will think exactly the same way as you or have the same values as you.

Something that seems unfamiliar to you might be normal to others.

A worldview is all the values, beliefs, and expectations that make up how someone sees the world. Having a wider understanding of worldviews can help us be more accepting of other people.

Respecting Others

One of the best ways you can show others that they matter is by giving them respect. Respect means being thoughtful and polite, not judgemental or rude.

You can disagree with someone and still show them respect.

What Does Respect Look Like?

- Asking questions to understand people better
- Listening without interrupting
- Speaking kindly to people
- Thinking about how your actions affect others
- Not forcing people to do things your way
- Treating everyone equally
- Not stereotyping people

Different cultures may show respect differently.

Understanding Others

When you understand why people think the way they do, it helps you understand how they feel. Understanding and caring for how others feel is called having empathy. Empathy helps us to be kinder.

People often show their emotions with their bodies and faces. If you notice that someone looks upset or angry, treat that person with kindness and respect.

Has anyone ever shown you kindness when you were upset?

Look Out For Each Other

Unfortunately, people are not always shown kindness. Sometimes, people get mistreated or bullied. You should never treat others in a way that you know is hurtful, even if others are doing it.

Bullying is never OK.

Sometimes, people who are being bullied might find it hard to stand up for themselves. If you see someone being bullied, you can look out for them by telling an adult you trust.

Build Up or Break Down?

It is normal to want to be good at everything. When you see other people doing better than you, you might feel jealous. Jealousy can be hard to overcome.

When you feel jealous, you have a choice. You can stay upset, or you can choose to be excited for the other person. Celebrating other people's success can boost everyone's mood.

Judging Others

Sometimes it seems like all we see is the worst in others. Just remember that everyone is human. Nobody is perfect. We all have things we could be better at.

Before judging others, think about yourself. What are you good at? What do you need to work on?

How would you feel if people judged you instead of showing kindness?

Healthy Habits

It can take time and effort to develop a good attitude toward others, but it is possible. It helps to plan out healthy habits to practice at school, at home, and in your community.

Habits are things that people do often.

In Your Home

Keep a diary of the good memories you have made with others.

In Your School

Look out for students who are being bullied. Help your classmates understand why bullying is wrong.

In Your Community

Learn about the different lifestyles, religions, and cultures of people in your area.

People Matter!

Everyone is important—your friends, family, classmates, neighbors, and even people on the other side of the planet. You play a big part in other people's lives, so having the right attitude toward them matters.

When everyone treats others the way they would like to be treated themselves, the world can be a wonderful place!

So, remember— be respectful to everyone and practice kindness wherever you go, because others matter.

Glossary

community a group of people who are connected by something

cultures the traditions, ideas, and ways of life of groups of people

diverse having to do with different kinds of people

expectations the beliefs someone has about how things should be or what will happen

judgemental filled with powerful, often disapproving feelings that someone is not acting the right way

religions systems of faith and worship, especially to do with a god or gods

stereotyping assuming that people from a certain group are all the same or act in the same ways; these can often be untrue

unique totally different from anyone or anything else

values beliefs that are seen as especially important in shaping who you are

Index